Read for a Better World™

# STEGOSAURUS

## A First Look

TOM JACKSON

Lerner Publications ◆ Minneapolis

# Educator Toolbox

Reading books is a great way for kids to express what they're interested in. Before reading this title, ask the reader these questions:

> What do you think this book is about? Look at the cover for clues.
>
> What do you already know about this dinosaur?
>
> What do you want to learn about this dinosaur?

## Let's Read Together

Encourage the reader to use the pictures to understand the text.

Point out when the reader successfully sounds out a word.

Praise the reader for recognizing sight words such as *was* and *had*.

# TABLE OF CONTENTS

## Stegosaurus

Stegosaurus is a kind of dinosaur. It lived one hundred and fifty-five million years ago.

**Stegosaurus**
**steh-guh-SAW-ruhs**

The dinosaur was as tall as a giraffe. It was as heavy as two giraffes.

The dinosaur
had a round body.
It had pointy
plates on its back.

How many legs does a stegosaurus have?

The back plates were made of bone and skin.

The plates helped the dinosaur stay warm.

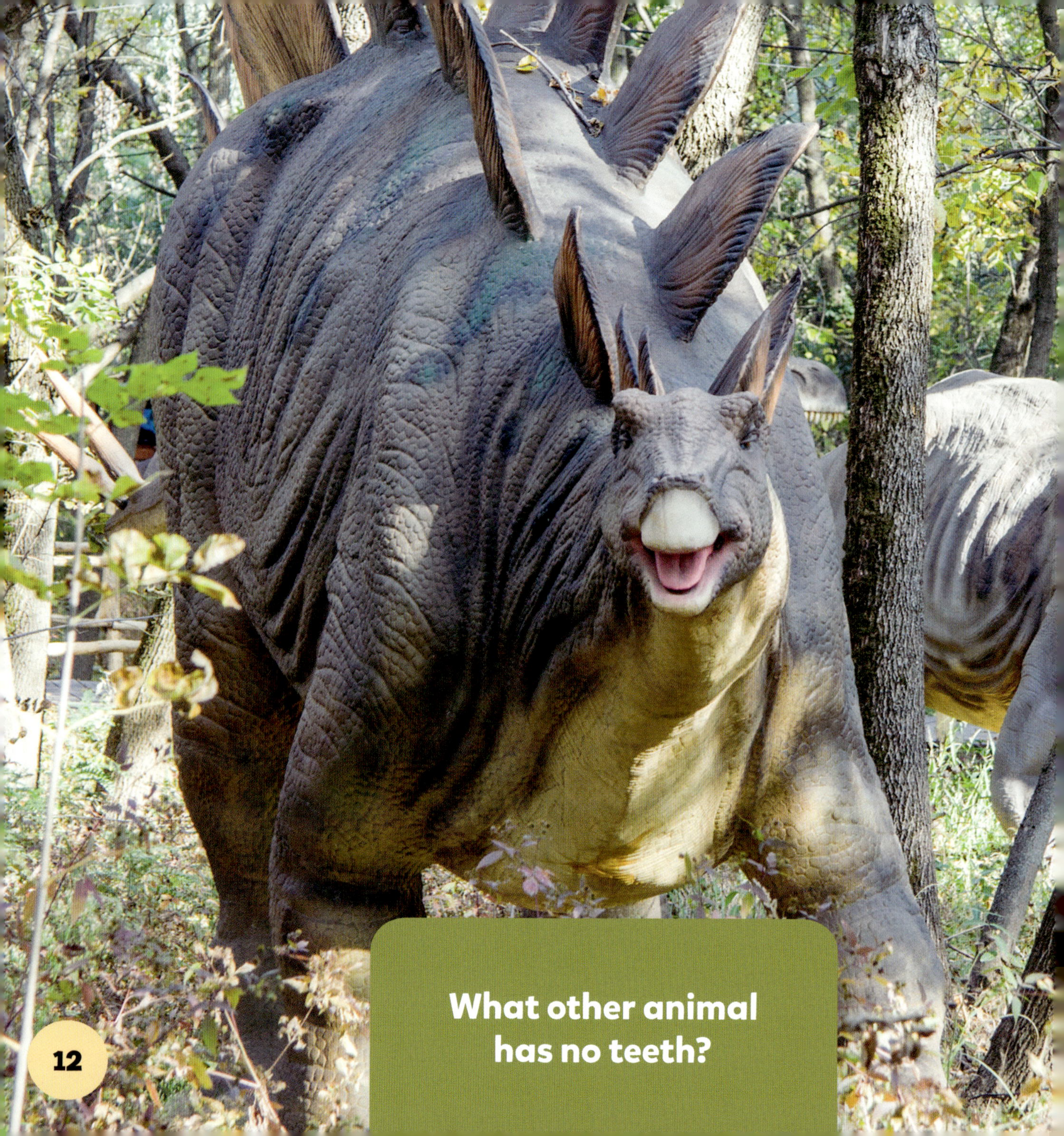

**What other animal has no teeth?**

The dinosaur had
a small head.
It had no teeth.

Its tail had spikes at the end.

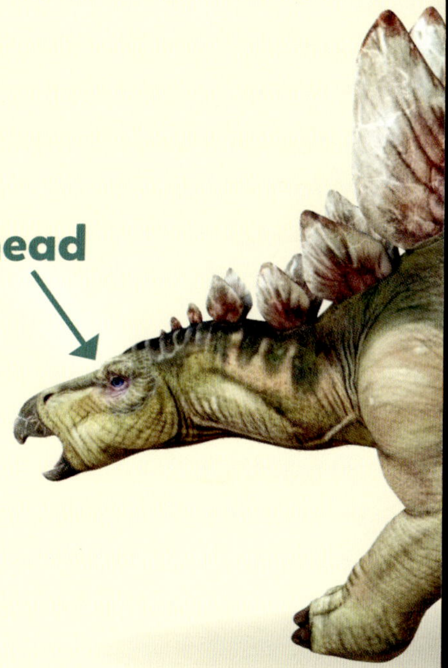

plate
spike
tail

Other animals attacked the dinosaur. It hit attackers with its tail.

What other animals eat plants?

The dinosaur ate leaves and twigs.

The dinosaur's bones help us learn how it lived.

## You Connect!

What is something you like about this dinosaur?

What else is as big as this dinosaur?

What other dinosaurs do you know about?

## STEM Snapshot

Encourage students to think and ask questions like scientists. Ask the reader:

What is something you learned about this dinosaur?

What is something you noticed in the pictures of the dinosaur?

What is something you still don't know about this dinosaur?

# Photo Glossary

giraffe

plates

spikes

twigs

# Learn More

Chanez, Katie. *Stegosaurus*. Minneapolis: Jump!, Inc., 2026.

Dittmer, Loris. *Stegosaurus*. Mankato, MN: Creative Education and Creative Paperbacks, 2024.

Giedd, Steph. *Stegosaurus*. Minneapolis: Kids Core, 2024.

# Index



## Photo Acknowledgments

The images in this book are used with the permission of: © Warpaint/Shutterstock Images, pp. 4–5; © Michael Rosskothen/Shutterstock Images, p. 6; © Andy Soloman/Shutterstock Images, pp. 7, 23 (giraffe); © Vladimir Bolokh/Shutterstock Images, pp. 9, 18, 23 (twigs); © kamomeen/Shutterstock Images, pp. 10, 23 (plates); © Toriz/Shutterstock Images, p. 11; © Viovita/Dreamstime.com, p. 12; © Daniel Eskridge/Shutterstock Images, p. 13; © KinoMasterskaya/Shutterstock Images, pp. 14–15; © Kitti Kahotong/Dreamstime.com, pp. 16–17, 23 (spikes); © oasisamuelShutterstock Images, p. 20.

Cover Photograph: © Daniel Eskridge/Shutterstock Images

Design Elements: © Mighty Media, Inc.



Lerner Publications Company
An imprint of Lerner Publishing Group, Inc.
241 First Avenue North
Minneapolis, MN 55401 USA

For reading levels and more information, look up this title at www.lernerbooks.com.

Main body text set in Mikado a Medium.
Typeface provided by Hannes von Doehren.

**Library of Congress Cataloging-in-Publication Data**

Names: Jackson, Tom, 1972–author
Title: Stegosaurus : a first look / Tom Jackson.
Description: Minneapolis : Lerner Publications, 2026. | Series: Read for a better world. Read about dinosaurs | Includes bibliographical references and index. | Audience: Ages 5–8 | Audience: Grades K–1 | Summary: "With spikes on its tail and plates on its back, the stegosaurus is one tough dinosaur. Photorealistic images and engaging text support young readers while learning about this cool dino"—Provided by publisher.
Identifiers: LCCN 2025011284 (print) | LCCN 2025011285 (ebook) | ISBN 9798765689790 library binding | ISBN 9798348029050 paperback | ISBN 9798765697627 epub
Subjects: LCSH: Stegosaurus—Juvenile literature
Classification: LCC QE862.O65 J2945 2026 (print) | LCC QE862.O65 (ebook) | DDC 567.9153–dc23/eng/20250630

LC record available at https://lccn.loc.gov/2025011284
LC ebook record available at https://lccn.loc.gov/2025011285

Manufactured in the United States of America
1 - CG - 12/15/25